USDA

U.S. Department of Agriculture
Office of Inspector General

I0426037

Compilation of Prior Inspector General Reports on International Trade and Competitiveness

May 2011

United States Department of Agriculture

Office of Inspector General

Washington, D.C. 20250

May 27, 2011

The Honorable Phyllis Fong
Chairperson
Council of the Inspectors General on Integrity and Efficiency
1717 H Street, NW.
Washington, D.C. 20006

Dear Ms. Fong:

Enclosed is the Department of Agriculture (USDA) Office of Inspector General (OIG) report entitled, *Compilation of Prior Inspector General Reports on International Trade and Competitiveness*. The USDA OIG led this effort on behalf of the Council of the Inspectors General on Integrity and Efficiency (CIGIE), based on a project plan approved by the Executive Council and subsequently agreed to by the full Council in April 2011.

In March 2011, the President tasked the Chief Performance Officer, who also serves as the Deputy Director of Management, Office of Management and Budget, to conduct a comprehensive review of the Federal agencies and programs involved in trade and competitiveness. The Inspector General community is in a unique position to provide valuable information to policymakers on the efficiency and effectiveness of current trade and export programs. Accordingly, CIGIE created an interdisciplinary International Trade and Competitiveness Working Group (Working Group). The Working Group compiled audits, studies, evaluations, inspections, and other reviews performed during the last 5 years in departmental/agency mission areas related to trade and competiveness and identified areas of program inefficiency, duplication, and overlap.

The report includes summaries of prior OIG work on trade and competitiveness, in an effort to provide a succinct overview of the wide variety of identified issues that could adversely affect our Government's critical activities related to international trade. The majority of Working Group submissions identified inefficiencies, lack of clear program goals and strategies, and poor coordination and communication among various agencies involved in trade and competitiveness. A few Inspectors General addressed issues specifically related to duplication and overlap of Federal trade functions.

The report contains no formal recommendations and is provided for informational purposes only. The Executive Council approved the report on May 20, 2011. We then provided the report to the

Inspector General community for review and comment. The final report includes resolution of the comments received.

We would like to thank the staff from across the OIG community who contributed to this report.

David Gray /s/ (Gil H. Harden, Assistant Inspector General for Audit, for David Gray)
Deputy Inspector General
U.S. Department of Agriculture

Table of Contents

Contents

Executive Summary

Background:

Both the President and Congress have cited an immediate need to eliminate wasteful spending and improve the Government's overall effectiveness by identifying and eliminating areas of redundancy in government operations. On March 11, 2011, President Barack Obama signed a memorandum to the heads of executive departments and agencies that established the first focus of this effort. Specifically, the President directed that a review be done of all departments and agencies having functions that "support one of our most important priorities increasing trade, exports, and our overall competitiveness ("trade and competitiveness")" by consolidating duplicate and overlapping functions. The memorandum tasked the Chief Performance Officer, who also serves as the Deputy Director of Management, Office of Management and Budget (OMB), to "conduct a comprehensive review of the Federal agencies and programs involved in trade and competitiveness." The President established a 90-day timeframe for the Chief Performance Officer to provide recommendations from this review.

In an effort to timely assist policymakers in their assessment of the efficiency and effectiveness of current trade and export programs, the Council of the Inspectors General on Integrity and Efficiency (CIGIE) created an interdisciplinary International Trade and Competitiveness Working Group (Working Group). The Working Group consisted of seven Inspectors General for the Departments of Agriculture (USDA), Commerce (DOC), Homeland Security (DHS), and State (DOS); the Small Business Administration (SBA); the Environmental Protection Agency (EPA); and the Export/Import Bank (Ex-Im). These Inspectors General responded to USDA's request for input from the Inspectors General of the various U.S. Government agencies involved in international trade. The Working Group identified and reviewed prior Office of Inspector General (OIG) reports on trade and competitiveness programs in their agencies.

Summary of Results:

The Working Group's objectives were to:

- Identify and compile audits, studies, evaluations, inspections, and other reviews performed during the last 5 years in departmental/agency mission areas related to trade and competitiveness.

- Identify areas of program inefficiency, duplication, and overlap.

As the Working Group compiled its submissions, we determined that there were additional factors adversely impacting the Federal government's administration of international trade and competitiveness activities. We expanded the criteria we identified to include fragmentation, goals/strategy, coordination, monetary, and security. A list of definitions for these terms is included at the end of the Executive Summary.

This report includes summaries of prior OIG work on trade and competitiveness in an effort to provide a succinct overview of the wide variety of identified issues that could adversely affect our Government's critical activities related to international trade. A table showing all the various issues, by agency, is presented below. Summaries submitted by individual Inspectors General describing those issues are provided as exhibits to this report. (See Exhibits 1 – 7.)

The majority of the submissions identified inefficiencies, lack of clear program goals and strategies, and poor coordination and communication among various agencies involved in trade and competitiveness. A few Inspectors General did address issues specifically related to duplication and overlap of Federal trade functions. We are including details on all the identified factors related to international trade and competitiveness, as we believe policymakers should have this information as they consider how to improve the effectiveness of these activities.

The following table identifies the types of issues reported by each of the Inspectors General in their reports on trade and competitiveness programs in their agencies:

Issue	Inspector General						
	DOC Exhibit 1	DOS Exhibit 2	DHS Exhibit 3	SBA Exhibit 4	EPA Exhibit 5	EX-IM Exhibit 6	USDA Exhibit 7
Duplication	X						
Overlap	X	X					
Fragmentation	X	X		X			
Inefficiency	X	X	X	X		X	X
Goals/Strategy	X		X	X	X	X	X
Coordination	X	X	X	X		X	
Monetary					X	X	X
Security	X		X		X		

As the table highlights, there are a number of factors, spread across many different agencies, that both individually and collectively have a detrimental effect on the United States' ability to increase trade and exports and manage overall competitiveness.

Trade Promotion Coordinating Committee:

Inspectors General of three agencies that have significant and critical roles in international trade note that improvement in the Trade Promotion Coordinating Committee's (TPCC) operations could assist in resolving several of the noted issues. TPCC is an interagency task force that ensures the coordination and development of a Governmentwide export promotion plan. TPCC is chaired by the Secretary of Commerce and the Under Secretary of Commerce for International Trade. It is made up of 20 agencies, with a core membership of 7:

- Department of Commerce
- Export-Import Bank
- Overseas Private Investment Corporation
- U.S. Trade and Development Agency
- Small Business Administration
- Department of State
- Department of Agriculture

The corresponding three Inspectors General that are members of the Working Group noted the following:

- The DOC OIG noted that interagency collaboration among TPCC agencies on specific trade promotion was not strong and the TPCC had not developed any working groups to improve agency coordination on this issue. The OIG further noted deficiencies in the TPCC's database for trade leads.

- The USDA OIG noted that the TPCC had not required USDA's Foreign Agriculture Service (FAS) to submit its annual accomplishments for promoting the export of U.S. agricultural products. As a result, USDA's performance goals and measures regarding exports could not be linked with the goals of TPCC.

- The SBA OIG noted that the National Export Strategy Report (Report), published by TPCC, did not describe SBA's progress in meeting specific internal trade performance goals or demonstrate how SBA's performance integrated with the activities of other Federal trade promotion activities. The OIG further noted that the Report was a backward-looking, rather than a forward-looking, strategic document.

Other Information:

As part of its planning process, DOC OIG identified the various U.S. Government agencies involved in international trade by function. We are including this information to provide the reader with an additional perspective of the numerous agencies and related functions involved in international trade (see Exhibit 8).

We also want to recognize the considerable number of reviews the Government Accountability Office (GAO) has performed relating to international trade and competitiveness in many of these same agencies. Those reviews are generally available on GAO's website.

Scope and Methodology:

USDA OIG chaired the Working Group that included six other OIGs who indicated that they had done prior work regarding trade and competitiveness. These included Inspectors General from the Departments of Commerce, Homeland Security, and State; the Small Business Administration; the Environmental Protection Agency; and the Export-Import Bank. Each member of the Working Group assessed reports it had issued during the last 5 years. The reports resulted from audits, studies, evaluations, inspections, and other reviews performed.

The Working Group:

- Developed a set of criteria for members to use to analyze the prior reports of their respective agencies' trade and competitiveness mission areas.

- Identified any reported concerns and potentially overlapping or duplicate functions regarding trade and competitiveness activities within each agency and between agencies.

To develop a comprehensive compilation of prior OIG work on trade and competitiveness, USDA OIG solicited input from the Inspectors General of the various U.S. Government agencies involved in international trade. This report is based on information provided by the Inspectors General in response to this request.

This report is a compilation of audits and other reviews previously conducted by members of the Working Group. As such, this report, by itself, is not intended to meet government audit standards.

Definitions for Criteria:

We used the following terms as defined by GAO[1]:

1.) Duplication – Two or more agencies or programs are engaged in the same activities or provide the same services to the same beneficiaries.

2.) Fragmentation – Those circumstances in which more than one Federal agency (or more than one organization within an agency) is involved in the same broad area of national need.

3.) Overlap – Multiple agencies or programs have similar goals, engage in similar activities or strategies to achieve them, or target similar beneficiaries.

The following describes how the Working Group defined the additional criteria used:

4.) Coordination – Lack of or insufficient coordination of activities, information, etc., between segments of an agency or among various agencies involved in the same or similar functions.

5.) Goals/Strategy – Unclear or a lack of established goals or strategies to guide an agency in effectively and efficiently fulfilling its mission.

6.) Inefficiency – A regulatory, operational, or managerial weakness that hinders an agency from effectively and efficiently fulfilling its mission.

7.) Monetary – Concerns with the management of, or control over, loans or other credit programs and outreach activities to make exporters aware of program availability.

8.) Security/Safety – Issues involving control over the end use of a product or national security implications.

---

[1] GAO Report: GAO-11-318SP, *Opportunities to Reduce Potential Duplication in Government Programs, Save Tax Dollars, and Enhance Revenue,* issued March 2011.

Exhibit 1   Department of Commerce   5

Exhibit 1 – Department of Commerce

Response to the CIGIE's Questionnaire Requesting Information About Prior OIG Reports on Commerce Units Involved In International Trade And Related Activities

Department of Commerce Bureaus having trade-related responsibilities:

COMMERCE BUREAU	INTERNATIONAL-RELATED MISSION AREAS/FUNCTIONS
Bureau of Industry and Security (BIS)	Ensure an effective export control and treaty compliance system by regulating exports of dual-use goods and technologies and enforcing dual-use export controls.
Economics and Statistics Administration (ESA)	(Composed of the Bureau of Economic Analysis and the Census Bureau) Maintain key statistics on international trade and investment used by many stakeholders, including economic policy makers, financial market participants, U.S. and foreign companies, and Commerce's own international trade agencies
Economic Development Administration (EDA)	Indirectly promote exports by preparing American regions for economic growth; partner with International Trade Administration (ITA) to promote the National Export Initiative and attract foreign direct investment in the United States; and administer Trade Adjustment Assistance (TAA) programs to provide assistance to firms and communities that have been adversely impacted by trade.
International Trade Administration (ITA)	ITA has four business units, each with its respective missions: • **Trade Promotion and U.S. and Foreign Commercial Service (CS):** Promote U.S. exports, primarily by small- and medium-sized businesses • **Import Administration (IA):** Enforce trade laws and agreements • **Market Access and Compliance (MAC):** Eliminate foreign barriers to trade, investment, and business operations, enforce trade agreements, and inform U.S. firms of foreign business practices and opportunities. • **Manufacturing and Services (MAS):** Eliminate or prevent trade barriers and expand foreign market access to increase U.S. exports.
Minority Business Development Agency (MBDA)	Promote the growth and competitiveness of large, medium, and small minority business enterprises by providing assistance to minority-owned businesses and counseling on international trade issues when appropriate.
National Institute of Standards and Technology (NIST)	Provide technical advice to the U.S. Trade Representative and ITA during international negotiations on standards and conformity assessment issues aimed at eliminating technical barriers to trade.
COMMERCE BUREAU	INTERNATIONAL-RELATED MISSION AREAS/FUNCTIONS

Exhibit 1   Department of Commerce   6

National Oceanic and Atmospheric Administration (NOAA)	NOAA handles international issues related to oceans, fisheries, climate, space, and weather through its five line offices.
National Telecommunications and Information Administration (NTIA)	Formulate international information and communications technology policy, goals, and strategies, and advocate and advance U.S. policy interests and objectives in bilateral, regional, and multilateral forums and consultations.
Patent and Trademark Office (USPTO)	Develop and strengthen both domestic and international intellectual property (IP) protection

Agencies for which Commerce OIG has conducted audits, special studies or other reviews within the past five years: BIS, ITA, USPTO

General Reports on Department of Commerce Bureaus/Programs:

- **U.S. Dual-Use Export Controls for China Need to Be Strengthened, IPE-17500, DOC Unit: BIS, March 30, 2006.**

    Issue 1 – Program Inefficiency and Security:
    Condition: The current dual-use export control regulations do not prevent the Chinese military from receiving U.S. commodities that can be used in the development of conventional weapons.
    Cause: There is no regulatory basis to deny an export license application for items the U.S. has determined should be controlled only for nonproliferation reasons that potentially could be used to enhance China's military capabilities solely on the basis of military end-use if the item is not controlled for "National Security" (NS) reasons.
    Impact: BIS states it has a policy of denial for exports to military end-users in China, but the regulations provide only a limited range of items subject to the denial policy.

    Issue 2 – Program Inefficiency and Security:
    Condition: End-use checks can play an important role in helping to ensure that exported technologies are protected from diversion to unauthorized end users or end use.
    Cause: BIS is not aggressively monitoring potential diversions of export-controlled items from Hong Kong to China.
    Impact: Despite BIS' end-use check requirements for Hong Kong and the placement of an Export Control Officer in Hong Kong in March 2004, there were a low number of post-shipment verifications (PSV) conducted in FY 2005.

    Issue 3 – Program Inefficiency:
    Condition: There is no procedure in place to provide technical review of shipment confirmation documentation to ensure that exporters or end users are in compliance with license conditions.
    Cause: BIS does not require any form of technical review of the documentation submitted to ensure that it meets the requirements of the condition. Office of

Exhibit 1   Department of Commerce   7

Exporter Services staff stated that, although Licensing Officers have the opportunity to review the documentation, they rarely mark them for review.

Impact: Without a technical review to ensure compliance, the purpose of placing reporting conditions on the license is defeated.

OIG Recommended: a) Export Control Regulations and Policies Related to China Should Be Strengthened; b) End-Use Check Programs in China and Hong Kong Need to Be Improved; and c) BIS' Monitoring of License Conditions Could Be Enhanced

Management Response: Overall, management agreed with these findings.

- **Commercial Services (CS) China Generally Performs Well But Opportunities Exist for Commerce to Better Coordinate Its Multiple China Operations, IPE-17546, DOC Unit: ITA, March 31, 2006.**

Issue 1 – Program Inefficiency:
    Condition: Commercial Services (CS) China, with the exception of its Shanghai office, has few verification procedures in place to support its claimed performance results, which show yearly increases.
    Cause: Guidelines in the CS Operations Manual are not specific enough to provide adequate guidance on maintaining supporting documentation of the export success stories prepared by CS trade specialists.
    Impact: This is a recurring problem that the OIG has noted in several CS overseas posts. Before performance statistics are presented to Congress and OMB, CS must confirm they are reliable and meet the reporting guidelines outlined in the CS Operations Manual and without specific verification procedures, data reliability is limited.

Issue 2 – Program Inefficiency:
    Condition: Commerce organizations in China may not be running or cooperating as effectively as they could be.
    Cause: There is currently no one person in China, or any other Commerce overseas mission, with the undisputed authority to coordinate and organize the efforts of all the Commerce organizations represented there.
    Impact: Within the CS post, the senior commercial officer is the top official, but he plays an ambiguous role in relation to the other Commerce operations in China.

OIG Recommended: OIG made 35 recommendations to improve CS China operations, including revision of the CS Operations Manual and development of appropriate management processes and lines of authority to ensure that Commerce organizations cooperate effectively in meeting Commerce's many challenges in China.

Management Response: For issue one, CS Management disagrees with the OIG's application to CS guidelines, primarily, OIG's approach to client verification of the export success and the linkage between value added service and benefit to the exporter. For issue two, overall, management agreed with these findings.

- ***U.S. Dual-Use Export Controls for India Should Continue to Be Closely Monitored,*** **IPE-18144, DOC Unit: BIS, March 30, 2007.**

   Issue 1 – Program Inefficiency:
   <u>Condition</u>: The end-use check arrangement between Commerce and India's Ministry of External Affairs limits the checks' utility, and checks involving Indian government or government affiliated entities are not always conducted within prescribed time frames.
   <u>Cause</u>: BIS has not set clear and consistent time frames for two parts of its internal end-use check process: (1) initiating PSVs upon receipt of required shipping documents and (2) notifying the Ministry of External Affairs about end-use check requests.
   <u>Impact</u>: BIS failed to follow its end-use check criteria for two pre-license checks (PLC) that were cancelled, but should have been rated as "unfavorable" because the government entity involved failed to cooperate in the checks.

   Issue 2 – Program Inefficiency:
   <u>Condition</u>: BIS failed to follow its own criteria for some PLCs and did not adequately target post-shipment verifications to help determine whether diversions were occurring.
   <u>Cause</u>: Some BIS Export Administration licensing officers did not fully adhere to procedures for requiring exporters or end users to fulfill license reporting conditions. Some staff were not fully aware of the reporting conditions they were required to monitor and were not properly referring noncompliant exporters to Export Enforcement.
   <u>Impact</u>: Although the U.S. government is concerned about diversions of sensitive exports to programs involving weapons of mass destruction (either within or outside India), BIS did not adequately target PSVs to help determine whether diversions were occurring.

   <u>OIG Recommended</u>: 10 classified and unclassified recommendations were made to BIS. Unclassified recommendations urged BIS to, among other things: List all Indian entities that should be captured on BIS' Entity List, or determine how to better ensure exporter compliance with export license requirements; determine why persistent breakdowns in the monitoring process occur; require Enforcement staff to closely monitor licenses at specified follow-up time frames; recommend that exporters who do not comply with condition 14 be denied additional licenses; and refer all noncompliant exporters to Enforcement.

   <u>Management Response</u>: BIS agreed with many of the recommendations and disagreed with some.

Exhibit 1   Department of Commerce   9

- ***Commerce Can Further Assist U.S. Exporters by Enhancing Its Trade Coordination Efforts*, IPE-18322, DOC Unit: ITA, March 30, 2007.**

  Issue 1 – Program Inefficiency:
  Condition: Interagency collaboration among Trade Promotion Coordinating Committee (TPCC) agencies on specific trade promotion is not strong.
  Cause: The TPCC has not developed any working groups or other forums that regularly meet to improve interagency coordination on these issues.
  Impact: Trade promotion efforts are not as strong as they could be.

  Issue 2 – Program Inefficiency:
  Condition: Coordination between Commerce and State is not as effective as it could be regarding export assistance at the partnership posts.
  Cause: Commerce and State have discussed the partnership program extensively at the working level, but have never formally agreed on how the program should be coordinated and what their respective responsibilities are for supporting the commercial function at the partnership posts.
  Impact: Lacking such an agreement and corresponding guidance from Commercial Service (CS) and State management, some confusion exists among CS and State officers about their own roles and responsibilities to support the partnership posts and export promotion efforts in the partnership post countries.

  Issue 3 – Program Inefficiency:
  Condition: International Trade Administration's (ITA) internet trade promotion resources are not as organized as they could be.
  Cause: More could be done to clarify the decision-making responsibility for organizing Internet content within ITA.
  Impact: Many overlapping websites still exist within the bureau, requiring exporters to visit numerous sites to obtain comprehensive information on specific issues.

  Issue 4 – Fragmentation and Duplication:
  Condition: The database on the TPCC Internet portal only contains trade leads from CS overseas offices and from some State Department partnership posts. Several other TPCC agencies, as well as some other Commerce organizations, have information on substantive export opportunities that could be included in the TPCC trade lead database.
  Cause: Instead of aggregating these leads on one Federal website, these other organizations are posting trade leads on their own websites. Also, the TPCC database does not take advantage of available technology to allow for automatic notification of export opportunities that match a company's industry profile, which could be a useful tool for busy exporters.
  Impact: It makes it difficult for U.S. exporters to search for all relevant trade opportunities. Also, by not having available technology to allow for automatic notifications, exporters are not able to save time.

Exhibit 1   Department of Commerce   10

Issue 5 – Program Inefficiency:

Condition: CS' Advocacy Center oversees Commerce's operations at the five multilateral development banks. The Center's staff, along with the CS officers assigned to the banks and some U.S. Export Assistance Center (USEAC) staff, have taken positive steps to increase U.S. exporters' awareness of opportunities at the banks. However, U.S. exporters are not fully aware of all opportunities at the banks.
Cause: While most CS officers and many State trade agencies and other Federal agencies were aware that CS maintains personnel at each bank, many USEACs, State trade agencies, and exporters did not fully understand the trade finance and procurement opportunities at the banks.
Impact: Exporters may be missing out on needed or valuable opportunities that the bank offers.

OIG Recommended: a) Opportunities Exist for Greater Collaboration with Trade Partners; b) Commerce and the State Department should strengthen their cooperative efforts to support partnership posts; c) despite recent progress, ITA can further improve the effectiveness of its Internet trade promotion resources; d) identification and communication of trade leads should be improved; e) Commerce can better communicate opportunities at the multilateral development banks.

Management Response: Overall, management agreed with these findings.

- ***The Overseas Intellectual Property Rights Attaché Program Is Generally Working Well, but a Comprehensive Operating Plan Is Needed*, IPE-19044, DOC Unit: USPTO, July 17, 2008.**

Issue 1 – Program Inefficiency and Duplication:

Condition: The roles and responsibilities of the attaches in relation to the ITA's CS and the U.S. Department of State need to be better defined.
Cause: Lack of communication with U.S. Embassy staff.
Impact: Possibility that responsibilities could be neglected or duplicated

Issue 2 – Program Inefficiency and Duplication

Condition: Guidelines and criteria for program expansion need to be addressed, as do attaché training and program continuity.
Cause: Lack of a comprehensive operating plan.
Impact: Program expansion may be carried out incorrectly; attaches may not receive the appropriate training; and gaps in coverage and staffing may occur.

OIG Recommended: That the U.S. Patent and Trademark Office (USPTO) needs to better define attachés' roles and responsibilities, improve attaché training, ensure program continuity, and establish guidelines and criteria for the program's expansion. We recommend that USPTO develop a comprehensive operating plan for the overseas attaché program.

Management Response: Management agreed with this finding.

Exhibit 2   Department of State   11

Exhibit 2 – Department of State

Mission and Functions

Agencies Having Trade/Export/Global Competitiveness Responsibilities for Which Your Office Has Oversight Responsibilities: The Bureau of Economic, Energy and Business Affairs (EEB).

The Department of State's Bureau of Economic, Energy, and Business Affairs (EEB) coordinates State Department advocacy on behalf of American businesses and provides assistance to open markets, level the playing field, protect intellectual property and resolve trade and investment disputes. Within EEB, the Office of Commercial and Business Affairs (CBA) solicits regular reporting on what economic sections are doing to promote American business abroad. CBA works with U.S. Government trade promotion partners and U.S. embassies around the world to support American businesses overseas by providing commercial information and identifying market opportunities for American firms, advocating on their behalf, and encouraging entrepreneurship. There are no reports that this gives rise to overlap, duplication, or inefficiency.

Agencies for Which Your Office Has Conducted Audits, Special Studies or Other Reviews Within the Last Five Fiscal Years: The Department of State is the only agency for which OIG conducts audits, special studies, or other reviews.

General Reports on Department of State Programs

The executive summary of the March 2007 OIG report on "The Department of State's Role in the Promotion of U.S. Business Interests Abroad" (http://oig.state.gov/documents/organization/131071.pdf) found that "since 2004, when OIG formally recommended that EEB prepare a plan for staffing and supporting posts that do not have commercial service (CS) officer positions, there has been steady progress toward the goal of strengthening what had frequently been ad hoc management of the commercial function at many U.S. embassies and consulates."

The following paragraphs summarize results from various Department of State inspections.

Program Coordination

A review of inspection reports covering the last five years shows that there is generally good coordination on most issues involving international trade and export promotion programs. Duplication and overlap in the commercial, trade and export promotion functions have not generally been problems in embassies and consulates. In most posts where CS officers are present there is good cooperation and effective division of labor on policy and advocacy issues between the CS, the front office, and the economic section.

Exhibit 2   Department of State   12

Training

The Department has improved, and will continue to improve, the training and orientation of officers who support the commercial function, communication between non-CS posts and CS posts that support their efforts, and the performance standards of non-CS partnership posts. The Department's Foreign Service Institute offers a Commercial Diplomacy course three times per year at present. CBA teamed with the Commercial Service to offer several web-based seminars to overseas posts in early 2011 on export promotion and *Invest in America* promotion topics. More seminars are planned.

Information Technology

The Department continues to collaborate with CS to improve information technology links between CS and non-CS posts. As of April 2011, State has been unable to negotiate access to Commerce Department IT systems for State Officers at partner posts. As a result, State officers do not have access to client information and must rely on CS regional posts to provide it. State has engaged in productive strategic planning with CS and other U.S. Government agencies, acting under the interagency umbrella of the Trade Promotion Coordinating Committee (TPCC).

Interagency Coordination

EEB's efforts have led to a net gain for the key U.S. goal of effectively supporting U.S. business abroad; however, strengthening of the commercial function remains a work in progress. There are a number of areas where planning has not yet reached the implementation stage and where recommended procedural changes could still improve performance. EEB's campaign to strengthen the Department's commercial function was not specifically engineered to support small business, but small and larger business interests have collectively benefited from it.

Commercial Service Staffing

OIG inspection reports show that the real problem for international trade and export programs at most posts is not waste or duplication, but rather that the commercial service has reduced offices and staffing, while limiting travel budgets. State employees available to cover export promotion are spread thin.

The problem of insufficient staffing is explained in a 2010 GAO report on export promotion (GAO-10-874 August 31, 2010; http://www.gao.gov/products/GAO-10-874). According to the report, CS officials froze hiring, travel, training, and supplies, thus compromising its ability to conduct its core business. CS's workforce declined by about 14 percent from its peak level in 2004 through attrition – affecting both the mix and distribution of personnel. CS intends to rebuild its workforce, but lacks key planning elements for doing so, and its budget request has weaknesses that could affect its ability to meet its goals.

Program Funding

State provides approximately $340,000 to $400,000 per year in financial support to posts' business promotion and commercial outreach activities through a Business Facilitation Incentive

Exhibit 2   Department of State   13

Fund (BFIF). FY 2010 was an exception, as BFIF was allotted over $520,000. The large increase in FY 2010 can be attributed to the launch of the President's National Export Initiative and a significant increase in commercial diplomacy training.

Posts submit BFIF project proposals annually, totaling $890,000 to $1,000,000; as a result, a majority of projects go unfunded. In addition, BFIF supports regional commercial training for officers and local staff that is not fully reflected in the annual project proposal total from overseas posts.

According to the 2010 GAO study, State was unable to determine the FSOs and locally employed staff (LES) personnel costs associated with its export promotion efforts from 2004 through 2008. State estimated that FSO costs totaled $15 million in 2009. In addition, State funded small export promotion projects at posts which, with staff costs in Washington, D.C., brought total estimated State spending in 2009 to $17 million. This excluded LES costs, which, if included, would raise the level State spending on export promotion. According to 2010 State Department calculations, FSO and LES costs totaled $15.9 million.

Program Inefficiencies:

Condition: Without a CS presence at post some reports show that the level of commercial support for expanding U.S. business activities is insufficient; officers and locally employed staff (LES) have trouble keeping up with the growing demands of the American business community; and there is inadequate staffing to cover commercial and export activity. Providing CS services at partnership posts is an additional job for State officers and LES, who also fulfill other Mission and Bureau economic goals. In a survey of the amount of time partnership post staff spent on export promotion efforts in 2010, FSOs indicated, on average, that they spent over one-quarter of their time on this activity, and LES at these posts spent more than half of their time on it.

Cause: Inefficiencies stem from staff shortages and inadequate commercial training of officers and locally employed staff (LES).

Effect: The resulting lack of substantive knowledge leads to mistakes, lost opportunities, and mismanagement of time and resources. In addition to a decrease in the number of CS officers at posts, the reduction of travel funds for CS officers resulted in fewer trips to provide advisory and technical assistance to constituent or partnership posts.

CS Staff Lost from 2004 to 2009, and Planned Staff Increases in 2011 Type of Staff	Number of staff in 2004	Staff Lost from 2004 to 2009	Increase in Staff Based on 2011 Request	Net change
Foreign Service Officers	246	13	59	46
Locally employed staff	944	128	138	10
Civil Service	541	98	71	-27
Total	**1,731**	**239**	**268**	**29**

Source: GAO analysis of Commerce Data

Exhibit 2   Department of State   14

Issue: Program Inefficiency – Embassy Conakry:

Condition: Inadequate coverage of U.S. business interests in Guinea. Insufficient visits by the regional Foreign Commercial Service (FCS) officer because of the press of business at the regional embassy and travel in West Africa is inconvenient, expensive and time consuming.

Cause: Embassy Conakry does not have CS or FAS officers assigned. The political/economic officer and the locally engaged staff work on commercial and agricultural issues.

Effect: The local staff feels like the poor cousins. The Embassy does not have the benefit of the regional officers' experience, knowledge of priorities in Washington, or oversight management skills.

Issue: Program Inefficiency - Embassy Asuncion:

Condition: The U.S.-Paraguayan commercial relationship is healthy and expanding. The level of commercial support activities embassy Asuncion provides to U.S. business is insufficient.

Cause: Too few LES personnel to adequately cover commercial issues.

Effect: U.S. business may not receive the level of embassy commercial support that it should.

OIG recommended that Embassy Asuncion, in coordination with the Bureau of Economic, Energy and Business Affairs, ask the U.S. Department of Commerce to fund an additional commercial LES position. Post concurred and requested FY2011 funding from Department of Commerce.

Program Overlap and Fragmentation:

Overlap of responsibilities in embassies overseas is rare. Embassy Beijing, however, is a case in point.

A 2010 inspection of Embassy Beijing revealed overlapping responsibilities, lack of communication and turf battles between the ten economic agencies at post.(*Embassy Beijing, China and Constituent Posts*; Report Number ISP-I-10-79A, September 2010, Recommendations 8 and 9; http://oig.state.gov/documents/organization/149567.pdf)

Issue: Program Overlap and Fragmentation – Embassy Beijing:

Condition: Issues of poor communication and competition over respective roles and ability to influence policy between the State Department economic section and the ten other economic agencies represented at the embassy. Multiple meetings with the same Chinese counterparts and interagency rivalries hindered responsiveness to requests for information from Washington.

Causes: (1) Overlapping policy responsibilities and different views among Washington agencies represented in Beijing; (2)withdrawal of a State officer position from the US Trade Representative office in Beijing, and partial staff draw-down in the Treasury office; (3) interagency policy disputes; (4) numerous economic agency heads and section chiefs of equal rank; and (5) otherwise commendable initiatives to shape two strategic dialogues with the Chinese – the Joint Commission on Commerce and Trade, and the

Strategic and Economic Dialogue – sharpened competition among agencies over respective roles and the ability to influence policy.

Effects: Different agencies had multiple meetings with the same Chinese counterpart on the same issue; some memos to the front office lacked proper clearances; interpersonal tensions and rivalries among agencies impeded open airing of views in embassy meetings; risk of presenting different positions to the Chinese.

OIG recommended that the Ambassador hold agencies accountable for cooperation and ensure better communication procedures. It also recommended that Embassy Beijing and the Department ask the Department of the Treasury and U.S. Trade Representative to restore positions for one Department officer in each agency, drawn from existing economic officer positions. In the compliance stage of the inspection, the post implemented better coordination procedures between agencies, but cited budgetary and prioritization constraints against restoring positions.

Exhibit 3   Department of Homeland Security   16

Exhibit 3 – U.S. Department of Homeland Security (DHS)

Agencies Having Trade/Export/Global Competitiveness Responsibilities for Which Your Office Has Oversight Responsibilities: U.S. Customs and Border Protection (CBP).

- CBP is charged with the dual mission of securing the Nation's borders, while facilitating legitimate trade and travel.

- CBP will facilitate about $2 trillion in legitimate trade this year while enforcing U.S. trade laws that protect the economy, the health, and the safety of the American people. CBP will accomplish this through close partnerships with the trade community, other government agencies, and foreign governments.

- CBP collected an estimated $31.75 billion in duties, fees, and taxes during FY 2010.

Agencies for Which Your Office Has Conducted Audits, Special Studies or Other Reviews Within the Last Five Fiscal Years: U.S. Customs and Border Protection.

DHS OIG:

- ***Targeting Cargo Containers 2008: Review of CBP's Cargo Enforcement Reporting and Tracking Systems*, OIG-08-65, June 2008** (http://www.dhs.gov/xoig/assets/mgmtrpts/OIG_08-65_Jun08.pdf)

CBP's Cargo Enforcement Reporting and Tracking System (CERTS) is designed to gather data on cargo examination findings and report on how efficiently examination equipment is being used.

Program Inefficiency and Security:
Condition: CBP could improve its management and oversight of the development and implementation of CERTS. CBP has not updated the CERTS project plan, to include the scope of work, a detail implementation schedule for system design, development, and testing, and cost estimates past Phase 1.
Cause: CBP bypassed key Customs Standard Life Cycle reviews designed to ensure end-users have a properly working system and have received management's approval to continue the project.
Impact: CERTS project development was delayed and not fully available to end-users as CBP originally planned.

The OIG recommended CBP: (1) Develop, implement, and monitor an updated CERTS project plan that includes details of the work to be performed in each phase of the project; revised schedules for the design, development, testing, and deployment of all CERTS phases; and cost estimates and sources of funding to complete all CERTS phases; and (2) utilize the CSLC for all CERTS phases to focus on satisfying user requirements, including mandatory reviews to improve management's oversight of the project.

All recommendations were accepted for management decisions and have been implemented.

Exhibit 3   Department of Homeland Security   17

- *Audit of the Targeting of Cargo Containers 2009: Cargo Targeting and Examinations,* **OIG-10-34, January 2010** (http://www.dhs.gov/xoig/assets/mgmtrpts/OIG_10-34_Jan10.pdf)

Each year approximately 11 million cargo containers arrive in U.S. seaports. To manage the potential security threats presented by this large volume of maritime cargo, CBP employs a multilayered approach, including analyzing and reviewing shipment information and targeting and inspecting high-risk cargo. The Automated Targeting System (ATS) is a key component of this multilayered security strategy.

ATS is an enforcement tool that uses sophisticated automated techniques and algorithms to perform risk-based analysis of anomalies and strategic intelligence to indicate which shipments are high risk and require additional scrutiny and mandatory security inspections.

Program Inefficiency and Security:
Condition: Of the 391 shipments identified as high-risk and selected for review, 57 did not have enough documentation to support the decisions that were made. Therefore, there was no means of substantiating that officers properly or consistently followed procedures in waiving or examining shipments to keep dangerous goods from entering U.S. commerce.
Cause: Guidance on how to conduct and record physical examinations of high-risk cargo containers for biological, chemical, nuclear, and radiological threats is outdated.
Impact: Potentially dangerous goods and substances may go undetected because CBP officers use their own discretion and inconsistent processes to examine cargo.

The OIG recommended CBP: (1) Require port directors to maintain either hard copy or electronic documentation produced when conducting examinations, or waiving examinations of containers determined to pose a high risk of containing weapons of mass destruction for a period long enough to allow for independent review; (2) update and implement examination guidelines to specifically address terrorism threats and outline minimum procedures for CBP officers to follow when performing antiterrorism examinations, including specific procedures for inspecting for chemical, biological, nuclear, and radiological threats; and, (3) periodically assess the examination process to ensure that CBP officers are properly performing and accurately recording examinations in ATS.

All recommendations were accepted for management decisions and have been implemented.

- *CBP's Container Security Initiative (CSI) Has Proactive Management and Oversight but Future Direction is Uncertain,* **OIG-10-52, February 2010** (http://www.dhs.gov/xoig/assets/mgmtrpts/OIG_10-52_Feb10.pdf)

CBP's Container Security Initiative (CSI) is a program that uses risk-based analysis to screen maritime cargo for weapons of mass destruction before the cargo is laden on vessels destined for the U.S.

Program Inefficiency, Security, and Strategy:
Condition: CBP's CSI program has proactive management and oversight processes in place to identify and inspect high-risk cargo at foreign ports. However, local standard operating

Exhibit 3 Department of Homeland Security 18

procedures (SOPs) for CSI operations do not contain minimum essential information and clear guidance. CSI's Strategic Plan does not address how its program integrates with other international maritime cargo security programs; it lacks updated performance measures; and the Plan does not include a vision for the future direction of the program.

Cause: The Evaluations and Assessments Branch (EAB) confirms the existence of local standard operating procedures (SOPs) but does not ensure that minimum essential information about CSI operations is included. CSI's strategic plan includes outdated performance measures and does not describe how CSI integrates with other CBP international maritime cargo security programs initiated after the plan was published.

Impact: Minimum essential information and clear guidance in local SOPs is necessary for consistency. CSI's strategic plan and performance metrics guide the future direction of the program. Accurate and relevant performance metrics help inform decision makers and the public of CSI's progress and achievements.

The OIG recommended CBP: (1) Identify minimum essential elements for inclusion in every local port SOP and include these elements in the CSI program-level SOP, (2) Establish a process for EAB Branch to ensure that all local port SOPs include the minimum essential elements as stated in the CSI program-level SOP, and, (3) revise the CSI strategic plan to include the current strategic outlook of the CSI program, refined relevant goals and performance metrics to help guide and inform CSI's future direction, and the impact of other CBP programs and factors that may affect CSI's goals and objectives.

All recommendations were accepted for management decisions and have been implemented.

- ***CBP's Importer Self-Assessment Program,*** **OIG-10-113, August 2010**
  (http://www.dhs.gov/xoig/assets/mgmtrpts/OIG_10-113_Aug10.pdf)

CBP's Importer Self-Assessment (ISA) program permits importers to conduct self-assessments to verify their compliance with Federal trade requirements in exchange for decreased agency oversight and other benefits.

Program Inefficiency:
Condition: CBP has not clearly defined the purpose of the ISA program, developed appropriate program performance metrics, or issued the official procedural guidance necessary to implement the program. CBP's oversight does not ensure that all ISA participants have internal controls that demonstrate their ability to comply with Federal trade laws and regulations. The ISA program's organizational structure does not support consistent or effective oversight of ISA importers.

Cause: CBP personnel rely on either draft or insufficiently detailed guidance to implement the program. CBP circumvented its official process for accepting importers into the ISA program. Port Account Managers do not follow written procedures in performing their ISA-specific oversight responsibilities; National Account Managers and Port Account Managers do not adequately review the results of ISA importers' annual self-assessments.

Impact: CBP's understanding and implementation of the ISA program conflicts with what is set forth in the ISA Handbook, which could cause inadequate implementation and oversight of the program. Inadequate oversight activities could result in abuse of the ISA program by importers, potentially resulting in the transport of unlawful goods and loss of government revenues.

Exhibit 3   Department of Homeland Security   19

The OIG recommended CBP: (1) Establish policy and procedures that document the management controls needed for ISA program operations, including: the purpose, goals, and objectives of the ISA program; the performance metrics to measure the effectiveness of the program in meeting the established purpose, goals, and objectives; and the formal procedural guidance necessary to support consistent and effective implementation of the program; (2) Assess the risks to trade compliance associated with the current policies and procedures for accepting importers into the ISA program, and establish internal controls to ensure that risks identified are mitigated to provide reasonable assurance of ISA participants' compliance with trade laws and regulations; (3) Require Port Account Managers to follow the same policy and procedures for oversight of ISA importers as National Account Managers, or remove ISA program oversight responsibilities from Port Account Managers; (4) Establish policy and procedures to ensure that ISA importers' annual self-testing results are requested and reviewed for compliance with program requirements.

CBP accepted all recommendations; they will remain open until they are implemented.

- ***Improvements Needed in the Process to Certify Carriers for the Free and Secure Trade Program, OIG-11-25, March 2011***
  (**http://www.dhs.gov/xoig/assets/mgmtrpts/OIG_11-25_Mar11.pdf**)

The Free and Secure Trade (FAST) program is a commercial clearance program for known low-risk shipments entering the United States, which allows for expedited processing for entities that have completed background checks and fulfill certain eligibility requirements. FAST carriers are required to participate in the Customs-Trade Partnership Against Terrorism (C-TPAT).

Program Inefficiency and Security:
Condition: Highway carriers that do not meet the minimum security standards are certified for participation in the FAST program. CBP Vetting Center and C-TPAT supply chain security specialists do not always follow established procedures when vetting carriers for certification.
Cause: Security specialists approve incomplete applications for program participation and there is insufficient communication between C-TPAT and the Vetting Center regarding coordination of resources and requirements.
Impact: Certifying C-TPAT members whose security profile responses do not satisfy minimum security requirements could compromise the goal of the FAST program. Moreover, because supply chain specialists have up to a year to conduct an onsite validation, high-risk carriers that were certified could have up to a year to participate in FAST and receive program benefits. Inconsistent use of the established vetting process could increase the risk of granting FAST benefits to ineligible applicants and could compromise border security. However, Customs and Boarder Protection's initial enrollment process for Free and Secure Trade drivers generally ensures that only low risk drivers participate in the Program.

The OIG recommended CBP: (1) Require C-TPAT to establish and implement a process for supervisors to review decisions made by supply chain security specialists during the certification process to ensure that security profiles are thoroughly assessed and highway carriers meet all of the C-TPAT's minimum security requirements; and (2) Clarify the FAST

Exhibit 3   Department of Homeland Security   20

manual and supply chain security specialist standard operating procedures to ensure that layered carrier vetting process is conducted, and continue current staffing and oversight efforts to address vetting backlog and communication challenges between the CBP Vetting Center and C-TPAT supply chain security specialists.

CBP accepted all recommendations; they will remain open until they are implemented.

Exhibit 4   Small Business Administration   21

Exhibit 4 – Small Business Administration

Mission and Functions

The Small Business Act stipulates that Commerce is the principal Federal agency for trade development and export promotion and that the Small Business Administration (SBA) and Commerce should work together to advance joint interests in international trade markets. In response to this mandate, SBA's Office of International Trade's (OIT) mission is to: (1) enhance the ability of small businesses to compete in the global market place; (2) facilitate access to capital to support export trade; (3) ensure the interests of small businesses are reflected in negotiations; and (4) support and contribute to the government's commercial and economic agenda.

Under the Small Business Jobs and Credit Act of 2010, OIT was restructured to:
(1) increase staffing at U.S. Department of Commerce Export Assistance Centers (USEAC) from 18 to 30 employees; (2) create a regional export development officer at each of SBA's 10 regional offices; and (3) create an Associate Administrator to oversee SBA's international trade programs. Additionally, the legislation established higher loan limits for export loans, authorized the Export Express Pilot as a permanent program, established a grant program pilot at the State level to enhance international trade, and called for increased collaboration both internally and externally among governmental agencies.

OIT Services:

- **Export Trade Assistance Partnership (ETAP)**
  ETAP is an Extended Multi-Class Training that leverages local resources including Small Business Development Centers (SBDC), USEACs, the private sector, and not-for-profits. ETAPs are typically conducted collaboratively between an SBDC, SBA USEAC representative, and/or an SBA District Office International Trade Officer; and consist of one-on-one assistance. Participants are considered clients of the SBDC and partner USEACs who help provide customized strategy solutions.

- **Export Outreach Teams**
  Export Outreach Teams are designed to make SBA resource partners (SBDCs, Women's Business Centers, Service Corp of Retired Executives) aware of the international trade expertise (USEAC, Export-Import Bank, freight forwarders, international bankers, and the U.S. Commercial Service) available in the area, and to enhance communication and collaboration between resource partners and international trade experts.

- **Association of Small Business Development Centers (ASBDC) Training & Counselor Certification**
  SBA OIT in collaboration with the ASBDC provides an international trade training track for counselors at annual conferences. This training is being linked to an initiative to certify SBA resource partner counselors for international trade. OIT is collaborating with

Exhibit 4   Small Business Administration   22

the Department of Commerce and the Trade Promotion Coordinating Committee (TPCC) in the creation of an on-line testing mechanism that will lead to certification.

- **Client Referral Pilot**
  OIT, in collaboration with the Department of Commerce, is piloting a referral process for New-To-Export (NTE) companies interested in and with potential to become exporters by connecting them to the most appropriate local or national resource.

- **TPCC Small Business Working Group**
  SBA OIT chairs this interagency working group tasked to address low participation of U.S. businesses in exporting and encourage companies to export to more markets. The working group is broken down into four task forces focused on identifying potential Small Medium Enterprise (SME) exporters, preparing SMEs to export successfully, connecting SMEs to export opportunities, and supporting SMEs once they find export opportunities.

- **Export Management Company (EMC) Matchmaker**
  The SBA's *Export Matchmaker Trade Show & Conference* is designed to engage small business manufacturers, distributors and suppliers with trade intermediaries (i.e., EMCs, export trading companies (ETCs), brokers and trade consultants). EMCs and ETCs can provide effective, low-cost, and expeditious means for small businesses to enter foreign markets.

- **USEAC Management/Export Finance Counseling & Training**
  The SBA delivers its export loan program through a network of SBA Senior International Credit Officers located in USEACs throughout the country.

Loan Programs:

- **Export Working Capital Program**
  The program provides lenders guaranties of 90 percent on export loans up to $5 million to ensure that qualified exporters do not lose viable export sales due to a lack of working capital.

- **International Trade Loan Program**
  The program provides lenders guaranties of 90 percent on term loans up to $5 million to businesses that plan to start or continue exporting or that have been adversely affected by competition from imports. The proceeds of the loan must enable the borrower to be in a better position to compete.

- **Export Express**
  The program provides exporters and lenders a streamlined method to obtain SBA-backed financing for loans and lines of credit up to $500,000 (75 percent and 90 percent guaranties).

Exhibit 4   Small Business Administration   23

- **State Trade and Export Promotion Grants Pilot Program**
  The Small Business Credit and Jobs Act appropriated $30 million for 2011 and 2012 each for competitive grants for States to help small business owners start or expand exports.

OIG's Audit of SBA's Office of International Trade

- **Efforts to Assist Small Businesses Compete in International Trade, Audit Report Number: 7-12, January 29, 2007.**

  Issue 1 – Program Inefficiency:
  Condition: SBA had not surveyed small businesses or conducted any other structured information gathering activities to identify key international trade constraints that U.S. small businesses faced.
  Cause: Human resource constraints had allowed a vacant position to go unfilled within the Office of the US Trade Representative.
  Impact: SBA was not effectively meeting the Small Business Act mandate of ensuring the interests of small businesses are adequately represented in bilateral and multinational trade negotiations.

  Issue 2 – Program Inefficiency:
  Condition: SBA was not facilitating matchmaking activities between small business concern exporters and importers.
  Cause: Financial resources prevented SBA from establishing/developing a matchmaking portal system.
  Impact: SBA was not effectively accomplishing its mission of enhancing the abilities of small businesses to compete in the global market place.

  Issue 3 – Program Fragmentation
  - *Condition:* The National Export Strategy's report process did not report the agency's progress in meeting specific internal trade performance goals or demonstrate how SBA's performance integrated with the activities of other Federal trade promotion activities.
  - *Cause:* The National Export Strategy Report was backward looking and not a forward-looking strategic document.
  - *Impact:* The National Export Strategy Report process did not promulgate a coherent government-wide strategy for assisting small businesses in competing for international trade.

The OIG recommended SBA: (1) fill a vacant position at the Office of the US Trade Representative (USTR), (2) develop a plan to create an electronic matchmaking portal which would match U.S. small businesses seeking export markets with importing concerns, and, (3) ensure performance measures for international trade activities are integrated into the National Export Strategy Report.

All recommendations were accepted for management decisions and have been implemented.

Exhibit 5 – Environmental Protection Agency

Environmental Protection Agency's (EPA) Mission Regarding Trade, Exports and Competitiveness:

1.) Regulation of the production, use, export and/or importation of pesticides, chemical substances under Toxic Substances Control Act, ozone depleting substances, fuels and fuel additives, vehicles, engines, engine-driven equipment, hazardous wastes, plumbing products and scrap metal.

2.) Negotiation of free-trade agreements on environmentally-related provisions. Participation in development of trade policy; for example, EPA:

- Participates in the formal trade policy development process chaired by the Office of the US Trade Representative (USTR).

- Works through a range of international organizations (World Trade Organization, the Organization for Economic Co-operation and development, the World Bank and the United Nations) to address the nexus between economic and environmental issues.

- Is involved in the negotiation of new free trade agreements, and in implementing existing agreements.

- Plays a role in projects that implement environmental provisions under free trade agreements, including: North American Free Trade Agreement (NAFTA). the Commission for Environmental Cooperation (CEC), the Dominican Republic-Central America-United States Free Trade Agreement (CAFTA-DR), U.S.-Singapore Free Trade Agreement, Middle East Partnership Initiative (MEPI).

- Collaborates with the United States Trade Representative (USTR) and the President's Council on Environmental Quality to analyze the environmental impacts of new trade agreements, as required under an executive order of the President.

- Works with the U.S. State Department to help countries address potential environmental impacts of increased trade.

- Is involved in discussions regarding environment, investment, technical barriers to trade for Trans-Pacific Partnership (TPP).

- Works with and receives policy advice from the Environment Policy Advisory Committee on issues involving the environment and trade.

Exhibit 5   Environmental Protection Agency   25

- Participates in the North American Development Bank (NADB) and Border Environment Cooperation Commission (BECC), which assesses infrastructure needs in U.S.-Mexico Border communities.

EPA OIG REPORTS:

- ***EPA Needs to Comply with the Federal Insecticide, Fungicide, and Rodenticide Act [FIFRA] and Improve Its Oversight of Exported Never-Registered Pesticides,* OIG Report 10-P-0026, November 10, 2009,**.
  http://www.epa.gov/oig/reports/2010/20091110-10-P-0026.pdf

Issues: Program effectiveness and interagency coordination.

The OIG found that:

1.) EPA is not complying with the Federal Insecticide, Fungicide, and Rodenticide Act (FIFRA), Section 17(a), which is, in part, intended to notify the government of an importing country that a potentially hazardous pesticide was imported into that country. Specifically, EPA does not comply with requirements to provide notice to all countries importing unregistered pesticides. EPA does not ensure manufacturer compliance with FIFRA Section 17(a) notification requirements. Consequently, there is no assurance EPA is receiving the entire universe of export notifications in any given year. Finally, export data on unregistered pesticides are insufficient for tracking and analysis.

2.) Export notification practices and data requirements are insufficient to monitor for the potential re-entry of never-registered pesticides on imported foods or to determine whether a dietary risk to U.S. consumers exists. The safety of unregistered pesticides intended solely for export is not evaluated by EPA. Therefore, the risk associated with never-registered pesticides is unknown. EPA does not know the pesticide class, volume, use, or final destination of unregistered U.S. pesticide exports. EPA also cannot provide the Food and Drug Administration (FDA) and the U.S. Department of Agriculture (USDA) with information needed to monitor and detect pesticide residues from pesticides that have never been registered for use in the United States. Therefore, the extent of dietary risk from never-registered pesticide residues on imported foods is unknown.

The OIG recommended that EPA

1.) Comply with the FIFRA Section 17(a) for forwarding requirement or seek official Prevention, Pesticides, and relief.

2.) Develop and implement management controls to ensure EPA is receiving Facility Planning Areas (FPA) from all manufacturers as required by Toxic Substances FIFRA Section 17(a).

Exhibit 5   Environmental Protection Agency   26

3.) Develop procedures for reporting FPAS for information, including intended use information.

4.) Establish criteria to govern when the quantity and composition of a never-registered pesticide for export could pose an unreasonable dietary risk.

5.) Establish procedures to mitigate risk from never-registered pesticides, including coordinating information with USDA and FDA.

- ***Border 2012 Program Needs to Improve Program Management to Ensure Results*, OIG Report 08-P-0245, September 3, 2008**,
  http://www.epa.gov/oig/reports/2008/20080903-08-P-0245.pdf

Issues: Program efficiency and effectiveness.

The OIG found that:

1.) The current organizational structure of the Border 2012 Program allows it to achieve a collaborative relationship at the U.S.-Mexico border and address environmental and public health issues unique to the border region. The structure also creates opportunities for stakeholder involvement from local, State, and national groups, while providing the program with the ability to leverage diverse partners and create an effective convening mechanism to discuss border issues.

2.) However, the current management controls do not ensure that project and program results are documented or that the Border 2012 goals are achieved. Specifically, we found that Border 2012 lacks a systematic roadmap that defines the relationships between resources, activities, and intended outcomes. We also found a lack of management oversight regarding program progress towards meeting goals and objectives. For example, supporting documentation regarding program accomplishments was not obtained or reviewed by Border 2012 staff. Furthermore, the current performance measures focused on outputs rather than outcomes; several of the performance measures were not assessable. As a consequence of the conditions cited in this report, the Agency is unable to assess the environmental and health benefits actually achieved.

Note: While the Strategic Plan for Border 2012 in and of itself is not a document focused on international trade, it does have implications for NAFTA. One of the key regulations governing the U.S. Mexico Border Program is NAFTA. Due to numerous Federal agencies working in this area, it is possible duplicative effort may occur.

The OIG recommended that EPA

1.) Develop a strategic plan for the Border 2012 Program that describes how the program will achieve desired results. The plan should include the following components: a national set of goals, objectives, and measures; a list of internal measures used to gauge project and program success; a logic model, or other similar

Exhibit 5   Environmental Protection Agency   27

document, that accurately reflects outputs and short, intermediate, and long-term outcomes of the program; a description of how each component of the Border 2012 Program, including grants, collaborations, and partnerships, directly contributes to program outcomes.

2.) Develop guidance that outlines roles and responsibilities regarding how the Border 2012 Program (a) accomplishes each program goal, objective, and subobjective; (b) obtains and maintains supporting documentation for accomplished measures; (c) develops and monitors criteria for determining what constitutes their successful completion; and (d) assures quality of data provided by grantees.

3.) Develop and utilize effective performance measures that are quantifiable and measurable, particularly human health indicators, to track and report project program outcomes.

- ***EPA Needs to Improve Its Efforts to Reduce Air Emissions at U.S. Ports,*** **OIG Report 09-P-0125. March 23, 2009**, http://www.epa.gov/oig/reports/2009/20090323-09-P-0125.pdf

Issue: Program effectiveness.

The OIG found that:

> 1.) EPA's actions to address air emissions from large oceangoing vessels in U.S. ports have not yet achieved the goals for protecting human health. The Clean Air Act (CAA) provides EPA with the authority to regulate emissions from oceangoing vessel engines when these emissions cause significant harm to human health. For over 14 years, EPA has acknowledged that human health has been significantly harmed by emissions from these sources. Thus far, EPA has only regulated nitrogen oxides emissions from U.S.-flagged vessels. EPA has chosen to defer taking a position on whether it has authority to regulate emissions from foreign-flagged vessels, although these vessels account for about 90 percent of all U.S. port calls. However, after many years, EPA's efforts with the International Maritime Organization (IMO) have the potential to significantly reduce these emissions. In October 2008, the IMO adopted new international standards for oceangoing vessel engines and fuels. Still, EPA must work to establish Emissions Control Areas for U.S. ports if significant emissions reductions are to be realized from oceangoing vessels.

Note: Among EPA activities to achieve sustainable ports the agency works with the Office of the United States Trade Representative and other economic agencies in the development and negotiation of trade policies and agreements to help minimize adverse localized consequences associated with growth in international trade; and supports the State Department in working with the Senate in ratification of the London Protocol to prevent pollution of marine waters, which focuses upon ocean dumping of wastes.

The OIG recommended that EPA:

1.) Assess EPA's authorities and responsibilities under the Clean Air Act (CAA) to regulate air emissions from foreign-flagged vessel engines in U.S. ports, in light of the new International Maritime Organization Treaty, and report any shortfalls to Congress. EPA should include in its analysis key air pollutants emitted by Category 3 marine engines not covered by the IMO Treaty and show how the Agency will meet its responsibilities under the CAA.

2.) Assess the extent to which Emission Control Areas (ECAs) should be designated for all U.S. coastal areas, under the revised Annex VI provisions. For all areas where ECAs are needed, ensure that the appropriate application materials and supporting documentation are submitted to the International Maritime Organization in a timely manner.

- ***Improvements Needed to Ensure Grant Funds for U.S.-Mexico Border Water Infrastructure Program Are Spent More Timely,*** **OIG Report 08-P-0121. March 31, 2008**,
  http://www.epa.gov/oig/reports/2008/20080331-08-P-0121.pdf

Issue: Program efficiency and management.

The OIG found that:

1.) From 2005 to 2007, EPA took actions to implement timeframes for Border Program projects, reduce the scope of projects, and reduce unliquidated obligations of projects. However, EPA needs to make additional changes to the process it uses to manage the funds Congress appropriates for water infrastructure improvements along the U.S.-Mexico Border. In Fiscal Years 2005 and 2006, EPA awarded $35.1 million to the North American Development Bank to construct Border Program projects that could not be built until they were planned and designed, which takes about 2 years. Since 1998, the Bank has accumulated an unliquidated balance of $233 million because EPA awarded grants to construct projects before design was complete. EPA managers told us they provided grant funds in advance to ensure funds were available to build projects once planning was completed. EPA staff also said they felt pressured to obligate the money to avoid a reduction in program funding. If this process continues, between $34 and $57 million of the funds Congress appropriated for the program in Fiscal Years 2007 and 2008 will not be needed until Fiscal Year 2010 or beyond.

2.) EPA's Region 6 Border Program grant work plans did not include specific projects, measures, milestones, or costs associated with projects. The work plan for EPA Region 9's Fiscal Year 2006 grant included total cost of projects, but did not include sufficient detail about how much the grant funded for the projects. EPA requires that all grant work plans contain objectives, specific tasks, a schedule or milestones, project measures, and detailed budgets. When EPA

Exhibit 5   Environmental Protection Agency   29

awards grants with work plans that do not fulfill all requirements, there is an overall reduction in accountability for the projects and funding.

Note: EPA provided $626 million in assistance agreements (grants) for water infrastructure improvements (both drinking water and wastewater) along the U.S.-Mexico border for projects starting between Fiscal Years 1997 and 2007. EPA coordinates and works with the Border Environment Cooperation Commission and the North American Development Bank to ensure border projects are designed and constructed to achieve environmental results.

The OIG recommended that EPA:

1.) Assess EPA's August 2007 policy for the U.S.-Mexico Border Program to specify the actions EPA will take when the fund balance reaches the $140 million threshold of concern.

2.) Require the U.S.-Mexico Border Program to complete planning and design of projects before EPA awards any grant funds to NADBank for construction for the projects.

3.) In conjunction with EPA Regions 6 and 9, prepare a plan to expeditiously use U.S.-Mexico Border Program funding for immediate needs other than funding construction of projects that have not completed planning and design.

4.) Adjust future budget requests for the U.S.-Mexico Border Program to reflect funds that have not been obligated in prior years.

5.) Prepare grant work plans that include specific projects, measures, milestones, and detailed budgets to be achieved with grant funds.

EPA REPORT:

- ***Potential Export of Mercury Compounds from the United States for Conversion to Elemental Mercury, EPA Report to Congress: EPA Office of Pollution Prevention and Toxic Substances, October 14, 2009**, http://www.epa.gov/mercury/pdfs/mercury-rpt-to-congress.pdf*

Issue: Description of current and projected market conditions

Topic: Imports of mercury compounds into the U.S. and their uses.

Purpose, Scope, & Content: The Mercury Export Ban Act of 2008 (MEBA), signed on October 14, 2008, prohibits the export of elemental mercury from the United States beginning in 2013. MEBA does not ban the export of mercury compounds. The prohibition on export of elemental mercury is intended to reduce the availability of elemental mercury on the global market.

Exhibit 5   Environmental Protection Agency   30

This report is submitted to Congress regarding mercuric chloride, mercurous chloride or calomel, mercuric oxide, and other mercury compounds, if any, that may currently be used in significant quantities in products or processes.

The report includes an analysis of the sources and amounts of each of the mercury compounds imported into the United States or manufactured in the United States annually.

The report concluded that elemental mercury will continue to be available in response to demand, particularly as demand from chlor-alkali plants and other industrial sectors continues to decline and secondary mercury from some of these facilities also becomes available. As a result, while supply and price fluctuations are likely, it is difficult to predict a scenario with the sustained scarcity of and high prices for elemental mercury that would be sufficient to support the development of the infrastructure necessary to develop and export compounds in order to provide an alternative supply of elemental mercury.

Exhibit 6   Export-Import Bank of the United States   31

Exhibit 6 – Export-Import Bank of the United States

Mission and Function:

Export-Import Bank of the United States (Ex-Im Bank or Bank) is the official export credit agency of the United States. It operates as an independent and self-sustaining executive agency and a wholly-owned U.S. government corporation.

Ex-Im Bank's mission is to support U.S. exports and jobs by providing export financing through its loan, guarantee and insurance programs in cases where the private sector is unable or unwilling to provide financing or where such support is necessary to level the playing field due to financing provided by foreign governments to their exporters that are in competition for export sales with U.S. exporters. Its authority to lend, guarantee, and insure is limited to a total of $100 billion. In Fiscal Year (FY) 2010, the Bank's total exposure stood at about $75 billion, up from about $68 billion in FY 2009. All Ex-Im Bank obligations carry the full faith and credit of the U.S. Government. The Bank's charter requires reasonable assurance of repayment for the transactions the Bank authorizes.

To provide the most effective assistance to American companies and increase the overall volume of U.S. exports, Ex-Im Bank is focused on:

- Expanding awareness of Ex-Im services through increased outreach and effective partnerships.

- Increasing the number of small and medium-sized businesses using Ex-Im products.

- Supporting environmentally beneficial exports, with a particular focus on renewable energy.

- Targeting business development to countries with high potential for U.S. export growth.

- Building expertise and tailor offerings to industries with high potential for U.S. export growth.

Ex-Im Bank is supported by the Department of Commerce's U.S. Commercial Service (CS), which operates 108 domestic offices at U.S. Export Assistance Centers (USEAC) and maintains 124 international offices in 75 countries that represent the significant export markets for U.S. goods and services. USEACs are intended to integrate the representatives and assistance of the principal Federal agencies, providing export assistance—the Commercial Service, the Small Business Administration, and the Ex-Im Bank. USEACs serve as one-stop-shops to provide exporters with information on U.S. Government export promotion and export finance programs and help potential exporters make contact with the Federal programs that may provide the greatest assistance.

Ex-Im Bank is a member or is part of the following:

- U.S. Trade Promotion Coordinating Committee (TPCC), an interagency committee created for the purpose of providing a unifying framework to coordinate the export promotion and export financing activities of the U.S. government and to develop a government-wide strategic plan for carrying out such programs.

- National Export Initiative (NEI), created to improve conditions that directly affect the private sector's ability to export.

- National Security Council (NSC) Interagency Policy Committee on Agriculture and Food Security (IPC), created to coordinate and integrate strategies.

- Interagency Committee on International Aviation Safety and Security, created to coordinate technical assistance in the areas of aviation safety and security in developing countries.

Agencies For Which Your Office Has Conducted Audits, Special Studies Or Other Reviews Within The Last Five Fiscal Years: Since the Ex-Im Bank's OIG began its existence in August 2007, we issued five reports that addressed international trade and export programs.

- ***Medium Term Export Credit Program - Credit and Fraud Risk Management and Business Process Improvement,*** OIG-AR-09-04, March 30, 2009
  http://www.exim.gov/oig/documents/MT Program Business Process Final Audit Report.pdf)

The audit found that Ex-Im Bank had not developed adequate customized policies, controls, systems, and tools to address the enhanced risks of the Medium Term (MT) Program.

Management described its decisions in setting policy for the MT program as reflecting the tension between potentially conflicting directives from Congress set forth in the Ex-Im Bank Charter: (a) take risks the private sector is unable or unwilling to accept, (b) provide for reasonable assurance of repayment, (c) ease the administrative burdens and procedural and documentary requirements imposed on program users, (d) render the MT program as supportive of exports as is the Bank's direct loan program, and, (e) obtain a broad participation of lenders in the MT program. In a number of instances addressed in this report, the Bank's management has responded to the directive to ease administrative burdens and procedural requirements by consciously abandoning or rolling back credit policies and requirements that other private and public sector lenders and credit insurers rely upon to manage fraud and credit risks.

The MT Program had significantly underperformed other Bank programs in recent years, accounting for a disproportionate share of credit and fraud losses. For example, of $965 million of MT Program transactions authorized in 2004 that were funded, approximately $256 million of claims for defaulted loans have been paid by Ex-Im Bank (reduced by recoveries of approximately $14 million). Approximately $101 million of these claims were associated with the publicly disclosed fraud schemes.

Exhibit 6   Export-Import Bank of the United States   33

To improve credit and fraud risk management and business processes, the report's recommended actions included:

- o Require on-site inspections and appraisals of financed goods/equipment as well as bank/brokerage statements to confirm borrower liquidity.

- o Establish an automated monitoring system and require more frequent remittance of borrower payments.

- o Formalize a lender oversight function for MT Program lenders.

- o Establish quality control processes focused on the MT Program.

- o Revamp the exposure fee pricing structure for non-sovereign transactions to more effectively price for the risk.

- o Consider moving away from a 100% guarantee for non-sovereign transactions towards more risk sharing between Ex-Im Bank and lenders to reduce "moral hazard" associated with MT Program transactions.

- o Standardize borrower submission requirements, including better defining what constitutes a complete application and creating a team responsible for processing more challenging applications.

- o Develop a strategic plan to provide stronger leadership and direction for the MT Program.

Subsequent to this audit, management agreed to the recommendations and implemented corrective actions.

- • *Medium Term Export Credit Program - Information Technology Systems, Support, and Governance,* OIG-AR-09-05, June 12, 2009
  http://www.exim.gov/oig/documents/MTITauditreportfinal.pdf

An audit of the efficiency and effectiveness of Information Technology (IT) support for Ex-Im Bank's Medium Term (MT) program found that the IT support, including level of IT investment in the Ex-Im On-Line (EOL) system, had not benefited from effective governance processes. The systems that support the MT program lack integration, functionality and embedded controls that are consistent with an effective transaction origination system. Insufficient use of systems development methodologies for business requirements definition, limited testing and lack of end user training throughout the design and build out of EOL and

Exhibit 6　　　　　　Export-Import Bank of the United States　　　　　　34

its supporting systems have contributed to EOL's performance problems, large number of change requests and defects and general end user dissatisfaction.

Ex-Im Bank management had not developed an IT strategy document for the MT program because a strategic plan was not in place for the MT program (or any other of the Bank's export-credit programs) or for Ex-Im Bank overall. Also, while Ex-Im Bank designated the heads of Export Finance and Credit and Risk Management as the executive sponsors of the new IT system, evidence such as formal meeting minutes was not available to indicate the frequency of or attendance at the executive sponsor meetings.

Significant enhancements to the Bank's processes for identifying strategic priorities, setting goals, developing plans to achieve them, supporting business process and system development, and allocating IT resources will be required in order to improve functional support for the MT program and create reasonable accountability for realizing management's objectives.

To provide adequate IT program support and governance of the MT program, we made five recommendations which management implemented. The recommended actions were:

- o Develop an IT Strategic Plan that is aligned with the MT Program business plan and covers the same time period.

- o Designate a senior manager with responsibility and accountability:
  (i) For management of the IT systems support for the MT Program
  (ii) To develop detailed business requirements for IT support of the MT Program.
  (iii) To facilitate effective communication and joint development efforts with Ex-Im Bank's Information Management Technology division.

- o Develop more fully functional support systems and data infrastructure, including the design and implementation of embedded system controls.

- o Develop data repositories that consolidate and organize the key transactional data fields, including eliminating existing duplicate files.

- o Make improvements to the systems development lifecycle (requirements, testing and training).

- • ***Export-Import Bank's Actions in Response to the Financial Crisis - Direct Lending,*** OIG-EV-09-02, September 30, 2009
  http://www.exim.gov/oig/documents/Actions in Response to the Financial Crisis.pdf

  Our evaluation showed that demand for direct lending from Ex-Im Bank had increased significantly since October 1, 2008, and that Ex-Im Bank responded to the international financial crisis by expanding its direct lending activity, enhancing its products, and adopting innovative structures to respond to the needs of U.S. exporters. Between

October 1, 2008, and June 30, 2009, the volume of direct loans authorized by Ex-Im Bank increased to $3.1 billion from $12 million during the same period of the preceding fiscal year. Total export credit authorizations for the nine months ended June 30, 2009, were $14.7 billion, compared with $7.7 billion in the prior period.

Additionally, although not part of the direct loan program, Ex-Im Bank modified its Working Capital Guarantee Program requirements for letters of credit and increased delegated authority limits to provide additional support to U.S. exporters, including small businesses.

We concluded that while the above actions were responsive to the international financial crisis and consistent with Ex-Im Bank's mission, opportunities existed to further improve the Bank's ability to respond to the current and future financial crises in the following areas:

o Management's ability to monitor and respond to market demand for particular services (such as the demand for direct lending during the current financial crisis) is limited because Ex-Im Bank does not collect relevant and available data in a systematic and comprehensive manner.

o Ex-Im Bank does not have a formal policy defining the substantive and procedural requirements that must be met to support the adoption of material policies, the launch of new products, or material changes in existing products.

o Ex-Im Bank does not have a documented plan to guide its response to the current financial crisis or other possible economic emergencies that might arise in specific locales around the world or more broadly.

The evaluation also identified need for Ex-Im Bank to improve communications with the U.S. Maritime Administration of the Department of Transportation (MARAD) and the understanding of Ex-Im Bank staff and exporters relative to the efficient management of U.S. flag shipping requirements. This policy, the requirement to use U.S. flag ocean vessels to ship U.S. goods in transactions receiving Ex-Im Bank support, has been cited by exporters as limiting the effectiveness of Ex-Im Bank support for U.S. exports.

We made the following four suggestions to strengthen the Bank's ability to assess the demand for direct loans as a result of a financial crisis and further enhance the Bank's performance and internal controls:

o Develop a systematic and comprehensive approach to collecting and reporting data relating to market demand and related factors impacting Ex-Im Bank performance.

o Adopt a policy for Ex-Im Bank setting forth clear written requirements for approving material policies, new export credit products, and material changes in existing export credit products.

- o Develop a plan to guide Ex-Im Bank's response to financial crises that is generally based upon evaluation of its response to the current financial crisis.

- o Actively work with MARAD to improve the efficiency of U.S. flag ocean vessel shipping requirements to minimize any negative impact on Ex-Im Bank support for U.S. exports during the international financial crisis.

In its response to our draft report, Ex-Im Bank's management stated that it was as well prepared as could be expected to respond to the international financial crisis. Management agreed that improvements were necessary to Ex-Im Bank's data gathering and indicated that it had undertaken a review of available options in light of Ex-Im Bank's staffing and financial constraints. Ex-Im Bank is currently reviewing the policy approval process to be sure consistent procedures exist for modifying or creating financing products. Management also noted plans to meet with MARAD to further discussions begun in late 2008 to address the issues noted in the report.

- *Sponsored Transactional Travel,* OIG-AR-10-04, June 04, 2010
  http://www.exim.gov/oig/documents/Sponsored Transactional Travel audit report.pdf

The OIG conducted an audit of sponsored transactional travel taken by employees of Ex-Im Bank during FYs 2008 and 2009. Ex-Im Bank has the authority to accept reimbursement from a non-Federal source for travel expenses incurred in connection to a Bank transaction. Ex-Im Bank generally complied with its established policies and procedures regarding the approval process, documentation requirements, and collection from sponsors.

While Ex-Im Bank's efforts were positive, we noted that improvements are needed in its policies and procedures to obtain travel expense reimbursement from the sponsor. We recommended that:

- o The Office of Administration and Security Director develop a policy and related procedures to follow-up on travel vouchers not submitted within the established time frame.

- o The Office of Administration and Security Director establish procedures to review travel authorizations for accuracy.

- o The Assistant Controller establish procedures to review bills for accuracy prior to sending them to the sponsors.

Exhibit 6   Export-Import Bank of the United States   37

Subsequent to our fieldwork conducted for this audit, management implemented all recommended actions.

- ***Evaluation Report Relating to Economic Impact Procedures,*** OIG-EV-10-03, Septembers, 2010
  http://www_exim.gov/oig/documents/EIB Report Final Complete Web.pdf

The evaluation determined that Ex-Im Bank's economic impact procedures can be revised to better implement the intent of Congress that the Bank's Board of Directors (not the Bank's officers and staff) decide economic impact cases. The procedures could also be revised to improve transparency and to make the economic impact review process more manageable for U.S. exporters and other participants. The small number of transactions requiring a full economic impact review that have been submitted to Ex-Im Bank in recent years may suggest that the Bank's approach to economic impact analysis has discouraged U.S. exporters of capital equipment from applying for Ex-Im Bank support.

Implementation of the suggested actions made in this Report should reduce the uncertainty, delay, and cost associated with transactions requiring economic impact review, and advance the Bank's mission of creating jobs for American workers by expanding U.S. exports. The suggested actions specifically addressed the following:

- o Improve economic impact procedures and reports to better support the Board's Congressionally mandated role in deciding economic impact cases.

- o Develop improved criteria to guide the Board and staff in deciding economic impact cases.

- o Improve the transparency of Ex-Im Bank's economic impact procedures and its economic impact determinations.

- o Improve the efficiency and responsiveness of the economic impact procedures by simplifying the process and reallocating resources.

The implementation of the 16 suggestions made in this Report will reduce the uncertainty, delay, and cost associated with transactions requiring economic impact review, advancing the Bank's mission of creating jobs for American workers by expanding U.S. exports.

Management's response to this Report states that management intends to consider the suggestions made in this Report in the course of its development of modifications to the Economic Impact Procedures based upon this Report and other sources of comments and suggestions, including ideas developed independently by the Bank's Policy and Planning Group (PPG), the 2007 report prepared by the U.S. Government Accountability Office (GAO), Export-Import Bank - Improvements Needed in Assessment of Economic Impact (GAO-071071) (2007 GAO Report) and "should coincide with the Bank's impending Congressional reauthorization."

Exhibit 7　　　　　　　　　Department of Agriculture　　　　　　　　38

Exhibit 7 – Department of Agriculture

Mission and Functions

The Foreign Agricultural Service's (FAS) mission is to link U.S. agriculture to the world to enhance export opportunities and global food security. Part of FAS' mission is to help provide outlets for the wide variety of agricultural products produced by U.S. farmers, thereby enhancing economic activity for agricultural producers. FAS serves U.S. agriculture's interests by expanding and maintaining international export opportunities, supporting international economic development and trade and science capacity building, and promoting sustainable development practices. FAS administers a variety of export promotion, technical, and food assistance programs in cooperation with Federal, State, local, private sector, and international organizations.

Market Access Program

FAS programs help U.S. exporters develop and maintain markets for hundreds of food and agricultural products, from bulk commodities to brand name items. The largest FAS promotional programs are the Market Access Program and Foreign Market Development Program. These programs are carried out in partnerships with agricultural trade associations, State Regional Trade Groups, State Departments of Agriculture, small and medium-sized businesses, and cooperatives that plan, manage, and contribute staff resources and funds to support these efforts.

Export Credit Guarantee Program

The Agricultural Trade Act of 1978 established the Export Credit Guarantee Program. The purpose of the program was to increase the profitability of farming and increase opportunities for the U.S. farms and agricultural enterprises by (1) increasing the effectiveness of USDA in agricultural export policy formulation and implementation, (2) improving the competitiveness of U.S. agricultural commodities and products in the world market, and (3) providing for the coordination and efficient implementation of all agricultural export programs.

OIG's Audit of USDA's Foreign Agricultural Service

- **Trade Promotion Operations, Audit Report No. 07601-1-Hy, February 2007**

Issue 1 – Program Inefficiency:
　　Condition: FAS does not formally track its efforts to expand trade activities in exporting U.S. agricultural products or outreach to U.S. exporters.
　　Cause: FAS abandoned prior efforts to centrally track such items as trade barriers because, according to FAS officials, the system was difficult to maintain and provided little benefit to the agency.
　　Impact: As a result, there is no assurance that FAS' outreach efforts are effective in expanding U.S. agricultural exports.

Exhibit 7   Department of Agriculture   39

Issue 2 – Program Inefficiency:

Condition: The 2006 National Export Strategy (NES) submitted to Congress did not present USDA's annual accomplishments for promoting the export of U.S. agricultural products or link information to USDA's Performance and Accountability Report.

Cause: This occurred because the Trade Promotion Coordinating Committee (TPCC), which is responsible for publishing NES, did not require FAS to submit this type of information.

Impact: As a result, USDA's performance goals and measures regarding exports could not be linked with the goals of TPCC.

Issue 3 – Program Inefficiency:

Condition: We found that participants do not conduct program evaluations on a set schedule.

Cause: This occurred because FAS does not have a mechanism that ensures comprehensive, periodic program evaluations are conducted by participants to assess MAP effectiveness. In addition, FAS officials stated that third-party evaluations would be prohibitively expensive for participants that received MAP funds.

Impact: As a result, participants cannot effectively measure their accomplishments with MAP funding.

OIG recommended that FAS: (1) identify those areas where tracking and analyzing specific data would be useful to the agency's efforts to expand exports of U.S. agricultural products, and, based on this documented analysis, implement a formal system to track this information; (2) ensure that organizations interested in exporting agricultural products are aware that FAS works through the industry trade groups to outreach to the organizations and provide information on foreign trade constraints and business opportunities; (3) work with TPCC to implement standard reporting requirements to provide a linkage between USDA's annual accomplishments and NES submitted to Congress; and (4) implement methodologies to ensure participants conduct periodic program evaluations to effectively measure their accomplishments with MAP funding.

All recommendations were accepted for management decision.

- **Export Credit Guarantee Program, Audit Report No. 07601-2-Hy, July 2008**.

Issue 1 – Program Inefficiency:

Condition: FAS implemented a risk-based premium structure for the Export Credit Guarantee Program (GSM-102) in July 2005 in an attempt to avoid $4 billion in trade sanctions imposed by the World Trade Organization (WTO). FAS' guarantee premiums were based on country risk; however, the risk of default is a combination of country and bank risk (i.e., the soundness of the foreign bank).

Cause: The country-based premium structure was chosen because it could be implemented in time to meet the compliance deadline imposed by WTO.

Impact: As a result, the premiums charged for GSM-102 guaranteed loans are not completely commensurate with the risks of making the loan guarantee.

Exhibit 7 Department of Agriculture 40

Issue 2 – Program Inefficiency:
Condition: FAS did not maintain adequate control over GSM-102 claim files.
Cause: This occurred because agency officials had not been designated with custodial responsibility for these records.
Impact: As a result, copies of documents used to establish valid claims against foreign banks could not be readily produced.

OIG recommended that FAS: (1) develop a new guarantee fee structure that includes the financial risk of both the foreign country and bank itself, and (2) develop and implement a records management system that complies with applicable departmental regulation (DR).[2]

All recommendations were accepted for management decision.

---

[2] DR 3080-1, dated April 30, 2004, requires that records be maintained and safeguarded so that they are easily retrievable and protect the legal and financial rights of the Government.

Exhibit 8

U.S. International Trade Function Chart

41

Exhibit 8 – U.S. Government Agencies Involved in International Trade by Function

Agency	Policy Development, Negotiations & Cooperation	Export Counseling & Assistance	Trade Leads & Market Research	Feasibility Studies	Finance, Insurance Grants & Adjustment Assistance	Advocacy	Inspection & Certification	Export Licenses & Controls	Import Admin. & Control
1. Agriculture	●	●	●		●	●	●		●
2. CBP	●						●		●
3. CEA	●								
4. Commerce	●	●	●		●	●		●	●
5. Defense	●							●	
6. Energy	●	●						●	
7. EPA	●						●		
8. Ex-Im Bank					●				
9. FDA	●						●		●
10. Interior (FWS)	●						●		●
11. Labor	●		●		●				
12. NEC	●								
13. NSC	●								
14. OMB	●								
15. OPIC		●			●				
16. SBA	●	●			●				
17. State	●		●			●		●	
18. TDA				●					
19. DOT	●								
20. Treasury	●							●	
21. USAID	●								
22. USITC	●								●
23. USTR	●					●			

Source: Department of Commerce Office of Inspector General analysis based on agency information.

CBP - Customs and Border Protection
CEA - Council of Economic Advisors
EPA - Environmental Protection Agency
FDA - Food and Drug Administration
NEC - National Economic Council

NSC - National Security Council
OMB - Office of Management and Budget
OPIC - Overseas Private Investment Corp.
SBA - Small Business Administration
TDA - U.S. Trade and Development Agency

DOT - Dept. of Transportation
USAID - U.S. Agency for Int'l Development
USITC - U.S. Int'l Trade Commission
USTR - Office of the U.S. Trade Representative
FWS - Fish and Wildlife Service

Exhibit 9   Abbreviations   42

Exhibit 9 – Abbreviations

AGOA..........African Growth and Opportunity Act
ASBDC.........Association of Small Business Development Centers
ATS.............Automated Targeting System

BECC...........Border Environment Cooperation Commission
BIS..............Bureau of Industry and Security
BFIF............Business Facilitation Incentive Fund

CERTS.........Cargo Enforcement Reporting and Tracking System
CPO............Chief Performance Officer
CAA............Clean Air Act
CBA............Commercial and Business Affairs, Office of
CS..............Commercial Services
CEC...........Commission for Environmental Cooperation
CSI.............Container Security Initiative
CEA...........Council of Economic Advisors
CIGIE.........Council of the Inspectors General on Integrity and Efficiency
CBP............Customs and Border Protection

DHS............Department of Homeland Security
DOC............Department of Commerce
DOS.............Department of State
DOT............Department of Transportation
DR..............Departmental Regulation
CAFTA-DR...Dominican Republic-Central America-United States Free Trade Agreement

ESA............Economics and Statistics Administration
EDA............Economic Development Administration
EEB............Economic, Energy and Business Affairs, Bureau of
ECA............Emission Control Area
EPA............Environmental Protection Agency
EOL............Ex-Im On-Line
Ex-Im Bank....Export-Import Bank of the United States
EMC............Export Management Company
ETC.............Export Trading Company

FAS.............Foreign Agricultural Service
FAST...........Free and Secure Trade
FCS.............Foreign Commercial Service
FIFRA..........Federal Insecticide, Fungicide, and Rodenticide Act
FWS............Fish and Wildlife Service
FDA............Food and Drug Administration
FPA.............Facility Planning Areas

Exhibit 9   Abbreviations   43

FSO.............Foreign Service Officer

GAO............U.S. Government Accountability Office
GSM-102......The Export Credit Guarantee Program

IA...............Import Administration
IMO.............International Maritime Organization
IPC..............Interagency Policy Committee on Agriculture and Food Security
IP................Intellectual Property
IT................Information Technology
ITA..............International Trade Administration
ITC..............U.S. International Trade Commission

LES..............Locally Employed Staff

MAC............Market Access and Compliance
MAP.............Market Access Program
MARAD........U.S. Maritime Administration of the Department of Transportation
MAS............Manufacturing and Services
MT...............Medium Term
MEBA..........Mercury Export Ban Act of 2008
MEPI............Middle East Partnership Initiative
MBDA..........Minority Business Development Agency

NADB............North American Development Bank
NAFTA..........North American Free Trade Agreement
NEC..............National Economic Council
NEI...............National Export Initiative
NES..............National Export Strategy
NIST.............National Institute of Standards and Technology
NOAA............National Oceanic and Atmospheric Administration
NS................National Security
NSC..............National Security Council
NTE..............New-To-Export
NTIA.............National Telecommunications and Information Administration

OIT..............Office of International Trade
OMB.............Office of Management and Budget
ORA.............Office of Regulatory Audit
OPIC.............Overseas Private Investment Corporation

PTT..............Permit to Transfer
PPG..............Policy and Planning Group
PSV..............Post-Shipment Verifications
PLC..............Pre-License Checks
PTI..............Priority Trade Issue

Exhibit 9   Abbreviations   44

SBA…………..Small Business Administration
SBDC………...Small Business Development Centers
SME………….Small Medium Enterprise
SSA…………..Sub-Saharan Africa

TAA………….Trade Adjustment Assistance
TDA………….Trade and Development Agency
TPCC………...Trade Promotion Coordinating Committee
TPP…………...Trans-Pacific Partnership

USDA…………U.S. Department of Agriculture
USEAC………..U.S. Export Assistance Center
USG…………...U.S. Government
USPTO………..Patent and Trademark Office
USTR…………U.S. Trade Representative, Office of

WTO…………..World Trade Organization

www.ingramcontent.com/pod-product-compliance
Lightning Source LLC
Chambersburg PA
CBHW080913290526
45795CB00007BA/2514